❧ Les ❧
Très Riches Heures

The Medieval Seasons

∽ Les ∽
Très Riches Heures
The Medieval Seasons

Preface and commentaries by Millard Meiss

Introduction by Jean Longon

GEORGE BRAZILLER NEW YORK

CATALOGING-IN-PUBLICATION DATA
for this book is available from The Library of Congress.

ISBN 0-8076-1399-1

Designed by Abby Goldstein
Printed and bound by A.G.M., Arese, Italy

Preface

There is luck in artistic creation, no less than in scientific discovery. A cycle of full-page illustrations of the calendar was the perfect theme for the Limbourg brothers in their mature years. In the choice the painters no doubt "participated," as Plato would say, together with Fortune. If, as seems likely, the idea of such a novel sequence was theirs, they would still have needed the approval of their patron, and he happened to be an extraordinary one. A series of Seasons was as rich in possibilities for them as the Life of the Virgin for Giotto or the Creation for Michelangelo. The Limbourgs were just then in the midst of great discoveries about the world and the means of representing it. Their contemporaries and successors in Italy, on the other hand, were far less concerned with the face of nature than with ideas and principles, and they never produced a memorable calendar cycle.

The calendar of the Limbourgs and, indeed, their entire cycle in the *Très Riches Heures* have become in our time one of the most famous of all works of art. Such wide popularity is absolutely exceptional for an illuminated manuscript that is closed in a library rather than, like other forms of painting, displayed in a public space. So familiar to us are the miniatures of the Limbourgs that we may be surprised to learn that they disappeared for three centuries without apparently leaving, during that time, any record of appreciation whatsoever. We know that the duke of Berry and the painters of the day greatly prized miniatures. The appraisers of the duke's estate fixed a relatively high price for the manuscript, which had been left only half completed at his death in 1416; in the early sixteenth century Flemish illuminators continued to pay tribute to the calendar pictures by imitating figures or entire compositions. Thereafter, like medieval art in general, the manuscript disappeared from history; in 1856 the perceptive founder of the Musée Condé at Chantilly bought it from an Italian family.

Though during the nineteenth century historians and collectors showed increasing enthusiasm for early Italian painting, the "primitifs français" caught on only a few years before 1904, the year of the first exhibition of French Gothic panels and illumination and also of the publication of the first monograph on the *Très Riches Heures*. French painting of the period came into focus much more slowly than Italian, in part no doubt because of the lack of a comparable critical tradition. There had been no Ghiberti in France to write sympathetically of the masters of the fourteenth century, and no Vasari to devise a systematic story of late medieval and Renaissance art. Thus only in recent years have we recognized the continuity of the French pictorial tradition from Jean Pucelle to Jacquemart de Hesdin, the Boucicaut Master, the Limbourgs, and Jean Fouquet; only now can we see that it represents a unique and vital phase of European painting, intermediate between the Mediterranean and the North and occasionally capturing the best of both.

By the imaginative selection of subject and setting, and by the sensitive modulation of light and color, the Limbourgs give us in the calendar a vivid sense of the world at different seasons of the year. The *April* and *May* pages depict scenes lush with fresh growth, the small trees bursting into bloom. The hot sun of *July* beats on the ripe grain and on the castle of Poitiers, giving each of its several walls a slightly different shade of white. Boys dive into the pond in *August*. The trees in *December* have turned russet, and fallen leaves litter the ground. In *February* the land lies covered with snow under a leaden sky. All life is controlled by cold. Outdoors, wood is chopped or transported; indoors, men and women toast themselves before the fire, the women raising their skirts for maximum warmth. Smoke winds from the chimney up against the icy sky. The snow has settled irregularly into the haystack (what perceptiveness!). The sheep huddle together in the fold, and the birds, caught without their usual food, peck at the grain previously scattered by a peasant, whose path from the house is marked by footprints in the snow. Altogether, nothing like this had ever been painted before, and, indeed, nothing like it would be seen again until Pieter Brueghel the Elder painted his beautiful oil-on-panel painting *Winter (Hunters in the Snow)* now in the Kunsthistorisches Museum in Vienna.

Here, in the *Très Riches Heures*, the penetrating light evident in all the miniatures led to discoveries that were momentous for Western painting. People and boats are reflected in the water, and shadows are cast on the ground. These are the earliest representations of such phenomena that we know. The shadows, furthermore, imply a single source of light, whether they fall behind the people, the scarecrow, the blackbirds and magpies, or the legs of the horse. One man even leaves his momentary imprint on the outer wall of the Louvre, anticipating by several decades the famous shadows on the art in Paolo Uccello's *The Flood*.

October is full of innovations of all kinds. The ground, instead of moving irregularly upward as it recedes, stretches straight inward. Nor does any road or line of trees curl back to measure and symbolize the recession. That is achieved by regular diminution, by overlapping, and by differences of color and tone. Indeed the brightest area is far away. Nowadays all this seems to us a rather simple feat, but no earlier painter, not even the Boucicaut Master, had quite achieved it. The scene, furthermore, has a new informality. Only the scarecrow and a tower suggest a central axis. There are no strong framing forms at the sides, and the two men in the foreground move out of the picture, in opposite directions. Never before had the continuity of space beyond the frames been so vividly conveyed. Finally, the linear perspective of the Limbourgs, though not fully systematic, helps to create imposing masses and traversable spaces—witness the enormous, four-square Louvre!

Indeed, the most memorable naturalistic landscapes in the *Très Riches Heures* are in the calendar, where they lie before a portrait of a particular château. In *April* and *May*, the nobles are framed by vegetation. Their place in the foreground conforms perfectly with their nature, tall, thin-limbed manikins in magnificent costumes. Their curling hats and trailing mantles weave enchanting patterns of rhythmical line and color. Only the peasants move into the countryside. They do so normally for their work; in other words, they apply themselves to the modification of the land. The courtiers could not possibly undertake this; neither they nor the religious figures in the rest of the manuscript were constructed for it. The ladies in *April* barely manage to pick flowers. The peasants are much sturdier. Still, we must admit that even they are not quite equal to their tasks. Perhaps this is one of those uncommon instances from which we may infer that an artist cannot do perfectly what he would like to do. The peasants do not easily wield their rakes, scythes, and sickles. Even in the masterful *October*, though the harrower is firmly seated in his saddle, the sower seems a little unsteady on his legs. Although the nobility and the peasants are very differently conceived, both of them have been idealized by the Limbourgs. The world is a garden, beautiful and secure, whether one hunts with falcons or mows ripe hay. The latter, it is true, requires physical labor, but in peaceful fields, under a bright sun. When the cold comes, as in *February*, there is a good fire—of which the unceremonious peasants can take greater advantage than the court in *January*. And it is country boys who slap in the water in *August* while the fashionable nobles ride in what must have been uncomfortably warm and confining garb.

It is clear, then, that in these respects the miniatures of the Limbourgs in the *Très Riches Heures* show two main pictorial modes, modes that are related to categories of subjects: agriculture on the one hand, the court and to a degree the religious on the other. Since we know from the entry in the duke's inventory that the manuscript was painted by "Pol et ses frères," and since we can safely assume that the style of each of these brothers changed during the several years of work on the book, no wonder there is no agreement about the share of the three nor, indeed, about the problem of authorship in general. Attempts to distinguish artists have, of course, been made; the dauntless Dr. Waagen, the first scholar to see the manuscript after its rediscovery in 1856, plunged right into a series of attributions. We owe the most perceptive observations to the remarkable connoisseur Georges Hulin de Loo, who in 1903 divided the miniatures among four masters. However, what Hulin did not notice is that all the calendar pictures showing the court turn out to be by his masters A and B, whereas those showing peasants he gave to his masters C and D. In other words, what I have previously described as differences of mode he assumed to be differences of hand. Of course, the two kinds of classification need not be exclusive, for certain masters may well have elected to paint certain kinds of subjects.

About 1485 Jean Colombe was invited by the duke of Savoy to complete the calendar and the rest of the manuscript. Colombe was a good illuminator, and since he worked in the style of Fouquet, who in turn had learned much from the Limbourgs, he was not an inappropriate choice for the task. Still, his role does not seem enviable, to us at least. Most of his additions, however, are not seen simultaneously with the work of his great predecessors, so that he enjoyed an advantage over, for example, a painter asked to finish another's mural cycle or a composer who had to complete another's polyphonic Mass.

But no later painter, however gifted, could have matched the smooth perfection of the Limbourgs' surface, their limpid color and complex simplicity. Their art could capture the delicate, fleeting beauty of a newly opened flower. As Emile Mâle, the noted art historian, once said: "Here is an instance where man was able at last to capture the transitory beauty of the world."

Introduction

The late fourteenth and early fifteenth centuries were a turbulent time of unrest and strife in France. Yet there lived one of the greatest patrons in the history of art, whose lavish and imaginative support made possible the illustration of two of the most exquisite illuminated manuscripts known today: the *Belles Heures* (The Cloisters, New York) and the *Très Riches Heures* (Musée Condé, Chantilly), both of whose miniatures were painted by the Limbourg brothers.

The *Très Riches Heures* was commissioned by Jean, duke of Berry (1340-1416), a great patron and friend of artists and a passionate collector; he loved sumptuous buildings, rare jewels, and richly illuminated books. Accompanied by his servants, chaplain, and artist, he moved constantly among the seventeen or more palaces, châteaux, and *hôtels*, or private city mansions, that he owned, some of which are depicted in the *Très Riches Heures*. Even his tapestries, decorated with historical scenes, were transported to adorn the walls of each residence in which he gave magnificent receptions for his family and retinue, served by his personal cupbearers, pantlers, and carvers, such as we see in *January*, the painting for the first calendar page.

A born collector, the duke was possessed by an insatiable curiosity and the desire to own everything that caught his fancy. His tastes were broad. He loved to own exotic animals; each one, including the Pomeranians that we see on the banquet table in the painting for *January*, had its own keeper, and the bears and their guardian followed the duke on his travels. Bears and swans were his emblems. The number of outstanding objects mentioned in his inventories is striking: histor-iated and emblazoned tapestries, Florentine and English embroidery, Luccan gold brocade, silk wall hangings, enamels, porcelains, and plates, forks, and spoons of silver and gold, all of which reveal the unimaginable luxury in which he lived.

The duke of Berry loved beautiful books, which he bought, commissioned, received, and offered as gifts.

Although his library was not as big as that assembled in the Louvre by his brother, King Charles V, the remarkable quality of his manuscripts established him as the prince of all French bibliophiles. He lovingly followed the execution of each page of the books he ordered, hardly waiting for the completion of one before commissioning another.

೦ఌ   ೦ఌ   ೦ఌ

Books of Hours, generally intended for private use, were the most popular devotional books of the later Middle Ages. This kind of personal religious manuscript became popular first in the fourteenth century, especially in France. Like the small diptychs or triptychs that were so common at the same time in Italy, the Books of Hours are striking manifestations of the new individual forms of patronage, of the concern with paintings for private prayer and aesthetic enjoyment. Even among manuscripts of this kind the *Très Riches Heures*, as it was called in the duke's inventory, was a very personal book. For the first time the patron enters into—even dominates—the previously generalized representations of the calendar, pages that appear at the beginning of the Book of Hours. The portrait of the duke at table in *January* is followed in the succeeding pictures by equally unprecedented portraits, if we may describe in this way pictorial replicas of fields and castles owned by the duke or by those related to him.

While the *Très Riches Heures* can be considered the most beautiful of all of the duke's Books of Hours, he owned others of exceptional interest, such as the lovely *Heures of Jeanne d'Evreux*, illuminated by Jean Pucelle (1325-28; The Cloisters, New York), or the so-called *Heures de Savoie*, begun in Pucelle's workshop, completed during the reign of Charles V, and destroyed in 1904, leaving only the fragment at present in the Library of the Bishop of Winchester.

∾   *∾*   *∾*

The Limbourg brothers—Herman, Paul, and Jean—were chosen by Jean de Berry in about 1413 to illuminate the *Très Riches Heures*, a Book of Hours to surpass all those he had owned until then. The Limbourg brothers were natives of Nimjegen in the Duchy of Guelders between the Meuse and the Rhine, it would be incorrect to call them Flemish; at the time, Paul was vaguely referred to as "alemant" or "natif du païs d'Allemaigne" (German or native of Germany). Records of the active exchange of gifts show to what extent the Limbourgs, especially Paul, enjoyed the intimacy and esteem of the duke of Berry, who bestowed on them the title of *Valet de chambre*. Upon the death of Jacquemart de Hesdin in about 1409, the Limbourg brothers seem to have succeeded him as Jean de Berry's official miniaturists. The consecutive execution of the *Belles Heures* and the *Très Riches Heures* (the first between about 1409 and 1412 and the second between 1413 and 1416) reveals the duke's insatiable desire, as soon as he had the latest book in hand, for another more beautiful, more sumptuous Book of Hours that would surpass all his others.

The miniatures of the Limbourgs and of their great anonymous contemporary, the Boucicaut Master, prove that in about 1400 in France major artists commonly undertook illumination. Indeed, their miniatures closely resemble panel paintings. The series of miniatures in this manuscript is thus like an entire cabinet of small panels. Like it, but yet not like it, for nowhere on earth is there a cycle of panel or mural paintings that still preserves the intact surface and the pristine color of the miniatures of the Limbourgs.

∾ *Plates and Commentaries* ∾

January

The duke sits at his table, surrounded by friends. Behind him the blaze of a large fire in the monumental fireplace is guarded by a wickerwork screen. Tapestries hanging behind the canopy depict knights emerging from a fortified castle to confront the enemy. The table is covered with a damask cloth and laid with platters, plates, and a splendid gold saltcellar in the shape of a ship. The duke's little dogs wander freely among the dishes.

A prelate with sparse white hair and a purple coat sits on the duke's right, thanking him for this honor. Behind him several figures are seen entering and stretching their hands toward the fire; the chamberlain encourages them, appearing to say *"Approche, approche!"* [Come in, come in!] Other figures complete this lively tableau, which re-creates a familiar scene at the court of Jean de Berry.

February

The Limbourgs chose a winter scene to represent this month, often the coldest of the year. They have painted it with extraordinary veracity, rendering details with a realism that captures the atmosphere of this harsh season.

Details in and around the farm are depicted with meticulous care: the sheepfold, the cart, the casks, the peasants and mistress of the house warming themselves by the fire. In front of the dovecote a benumbed figure clutches a wool coat over his head and shoulders as he hurries home.

The severity of the winter is further emphasized by the birds huddled near the house, scratching for food, which the snow makes it impossible to find elsewhere. Everything in this picture of winter is noted with care and rendered with skill, attesting to the painters' power of observation and the perfection of their art.

March

 The illumination for this month is the first of the great landscapes favored by the Limbourgs in the *Très Riches Heures*. It features the majestic Château de Lusignan, one of the duke of Berry's favorite residences.

In the upper left of the scene, a shepherd and his dog tend a flock of sheep; below them three peasants trim vines within an enclosure. On the right, another enclosure, with a house, seems to surround more vineyards. A small monument known as a *Montjoie* rises at the intersection of paths separating the different plots.

A beautiful picture of plowing occupies the foreground. A white-bearded peasant wearing a surcoat over a blue tunic holds the plow handle with his left hand and goads the oxen with his right. As always, each detail is rendered with extraordinary precision and delicacy.

April

Nature revives, flowers spring from the fresh grass. One and all celebrate this rejuvenation and become part of it.

The scene is at Dourdan, the property of the duke of Berry from 1400, improved and fortified by him. The towers and dungeon of the château, whose ruins are visible to this day, rise at the top of a hill.

In the foreground, two maidens bend to pick violets while a betrothed couple exchange rings before their parents. Expressions are rendered with subtlety: the fiancé searches the face of his betrothed while presenting her with the ring toward which she extends her finger and lowers her eyes. The mother is visibly moved; the father turns to look affectionately at his daughter. The Limbourgs have created a harmony of color, composition, and emotion that is perfectly attuned to the scene represented and to the charm of the new season.

May

"C'est le mai, c'est le mai, c'est le joli mois de mai!" [It's May, it's May, it's the beautiful month of May!] As the song of old went, so the figures of this merry pageant seem to be saying to one another.

On the first of May, young men used to make a light-hearted jaunt through the country to bring back branches. On that day, tradition had it that one wore green, as seen on the three girls riding horses in the foreground (the color in the manuscript is obtained from crushed malachite). The sumptuous dress lined with blue and ornamented with gold flowerwork identifies the girls as princesses. Turning to contemplate the one at center is a rider dressed half in red, half in black and white, the royal livery of France at that time. At the girl's left rides a man dressed in a rich blue brocaded coat strewn with golden flowers: could it be the duke of Berry?

June

It is harvest time; scantily clad peasants wearing hats mow the wide meadow in unison. Every detail is carefully observed and rendered: the freshly mown area stands out brightly against the untouched grass, and the already fading shocked hay is still different in color. The grace, even the elegance, imparted by the fragility and flexibility of the two, simply dressed, women reapers is typical of the mixture of perception and charm that characterizes the Limbourgs' genius.

The view encompasses the fields on either side of the Seine and the inner façade of the Palais de la Cité. The slate roofs of the Palais rise against a blue sky, providing a large, dignified background for this rustic scene; the minutely recorded details of this interior façade are particularly precious. On the far right is the Sainte-Chapelle in all its refined splendor. A boat on the riverbank completes this scene, to which the artists imparted both homely grace and grandeur.

July

The Limbourgs represent here rustic activities of the month of July, the harvest and sheep shearing, in the vicinity of the Château de Clain in Poitiers, which was one of the duke Berry's habitual homes. This miniature is a precious document of the château, which, sadly, no longer exists. We glimpse a chapel to the right of the château amid buildings separated from it by an arm in the river.

In the foreground two peasants wearing straw hats and drawers (called *petits draps*) reap with sickles. Every detail of the wheat is minutely rendered. The heads are more golden than the stalks, and both are speckled with flowers; on the ground lies mown wheat, not yet bound in sheaves but already drier than the rest.

At the lower right a man and woman proceed with the shearing with a kind of shears called *forces*; the shorn wool accumulates at their feet.

August

The scene is at Estampes, which, like nearby Dourdon, belonged to the Duc de Berry. A richly dressed horseman, wearing a white hood and bearing a falcon on his fist, leads two couples hawking. Leading on foot, a falconer holds two birds on his left fist and drags a long pole in his right hand. Behind him a rider releases a falcon from his right hand. The couple at the rear appear more concerned with an amorous conversation than with the hunt.

In the background, peasants bind into sheaves the newly mown wheat as swimmers frolic in the Juine River. The deformation of the figures' appearance by the water's refraction has been carefully observed and curiously rendered. All of this varied scene recalls the diversions of court life amid the seasonal work of the country. Thus we review, from one month to the next, the daily life of the court of the duke of Berry.

September

This depiction of the grape harvest features the extraordinary Château de Saumur, near Angers, which belonged to a nephew of the duke of Berry, Louis II, the duke of Anjou, who had completed its construction at the end of the fourteenth century. It appears here in all its fresh newness: chimneys, pinnacles, and weather vanes crowned with golden fleurs-de-lys thrust skyward. The château stands to this day, although its crowning crenellations have disappeared.

In the harvest scene (actually executed by Jean Colombe), aproned women and young men pick the purple-colored clusters of grapes and fill baskets to be loaded into hampers hanging from the mules or into vats on the wagons. Despite the slightly less refined style of Colombe, this harvest scene is one of the most picturesque and beautiful in the calendar.

October

October, the month of tilling and sowing, is represented along the left bank of the Seine. The view is from the vicinity of the Hôtel de Nesle, the duke of Berry's Paris home. Here, the Limbourgs show the Louvre, the royal residence since the time of Philippe Auguste (reigned 1180-1223). Every detail is so precise that even today, several centuries after the building's destruction, a model of it was made possible in thanks largely to the Limbourgs' painting.

In the foreground, a peasant wearing a blue tunic sows seeds that he carries in a white cloth pouch. At the left, a peasant on horseback draws a harrow on which a heavy stone has been placed to make it penetrate more deeply into the earth. A scarecrow dressed as an archer and strings drawn between stakes both help discourage birds from eating the seeds.

November

 The scene of November showing the acorn harvest was executed entirely by Jean Colombe. The Limbourgs painted only the tympanum, which—as in the other eleven months—crowns the scene with signs centered around a semicircle painted in blue *camaïeu* (monochrome), in which a man carrying a brilliant sun is enthroned on a chariot drawn by two horses.

Unlike the other scenes, this does not take place on a famous site that the artists were proud to evoke. The setting seems to be a figment of Jean Colombe's imagination. In front, a peasant dressed in a tunic with gold highlights, draws back his arm and prepares to hurl a stick into an oak tree. At his feet, pigs greedily eat the fallen acorns under the watchful eyes of a dog. On the horizon a sinuous river twists between the mountains.

December

With the month of December representing the end of a wild boar hunt in
the forest of Vincennes, we return to
the Limbourgs and the duke of Berry.
The scene features the home in which the duke was born
on the eve of December (November 30, 1340): the Château
de Vincennes, with its nine magnificent towers.

In the foreground, the boar has been run down and
speared by the huntsman on the left, and hounds are tear-
ing it apart. On the right, a hunter blows the mort on his
small horn. The dogs' desperate eagerness is rendered
with astonishing realism: the positions, the gestures of
their paws, their greedy expressions, all have been
observed and noted with care. This scene is perhaps the
liveliest in a calendar full of lively images; it completes the
year in an appropriate setting and time, recalling the birth
of the duke of Berry.